Content

Weekly Units

Further Unit Activities

ph as /f/

In some words, the /f/ sound is written as ‹ph›.

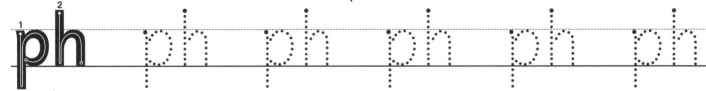

photo   nephew   graph

alphabet   microphone   orphan

pamphlet   phrase

Read the words below and draw a picture for each one.

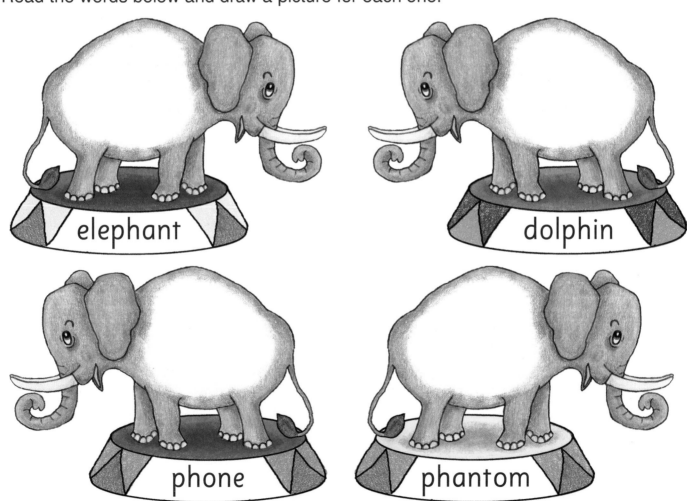

elephant

dolphin

phone

phantom

2

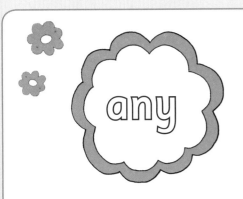

Tricky Words

any   many

Write over the dotted letters and add the missing letters.

any   a__y   __ny   an__   __n__

many   m__ny   __a__y   man__

Finish these sentences by adding either "any" or "many."

Have you got _____ milk?

How _____ ducks are on the pond?

Listen and write.

_____

_____

Read the tricky words and color the flowers using either red or green.

what   when   why   where   who   which

3

Words and Sentences

Read the list of things you might find out at sea and add them to the picture.

1. six fish
2. a big crab
3. three red shells
4. a starfish
5. a shark with big teeth
6. a flying seagull
7. a boat
8. a man in the boat
9. a yellow sun in the sky

4

Unit 2  Soft c

When the letter ‹c› is followed by ‹e›, ‹i›, or ‹y›, it usually makes a /s/ sound.

| race | city | fancy | mice | bouncy |

| prince | acid | cylinder | voice | accident |

Read each word below and write it under the matching circus tent. Color the pictures.

ice cream

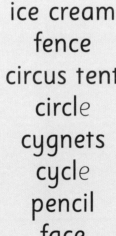

ice cream
fence
circus tent
circle
cygnets
cycle
pencil
face

5

 **more**

 **Tricky Words**

 **before**

Write over the dotted letters and add the missing letters.

more   m_re   _or_   mo_e

before   be_or_   __fo_e

Finish these sentences by adding either "more" or "before."

I went swimming _____ lunch.

"We need _____ butter," said Dad.

Listen and write.

_____

_____

Read the tricky words and color the flowers using a green pen or pencil.

why   where   who   which   any   many

Words and Sentences

Is it true? Write "yes" or "no" underneath each statement.

The cat is sleeping.

yes

Rabbits are good at hopping.

_____

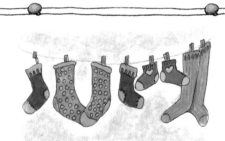

There are five red socks.

_____

It is three o'clock.

_____

The dragon has ten eggs.

_____

The magpie has a hat.

_____

Unit 3  Soft g

When the letter ‹g› is followed by ‹e›, ‹i›, or ‹y›, it usually makes a /j/ sound. Read the words and write each one in the vegetable with the same spelling pattern.

germ | giant | large | gypsy | vegetable

gym | ginger | magic | orange | energy

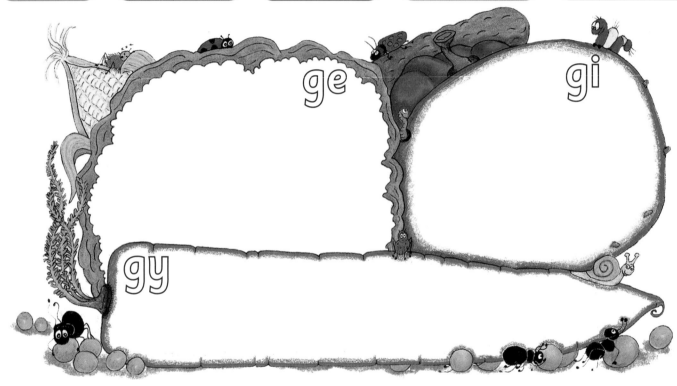

ge

gi

gy

Read the words and draw pictures to match.

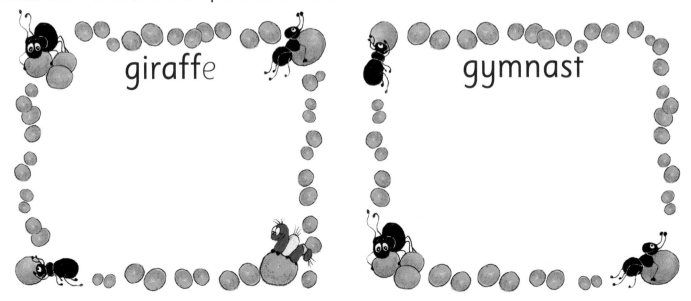

giraffe

gymnast

8

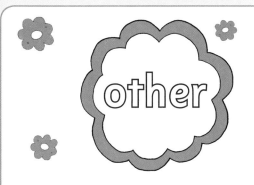
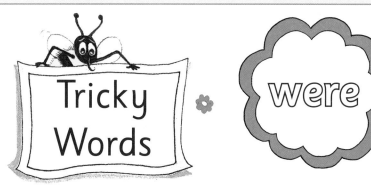
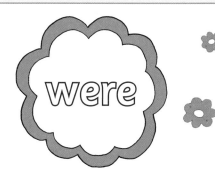

Tricky Words

Write over the dotted letters and add the missing letters.

other   o___er _ther _th___

were   wer_ _e_e w___e

Finish these sentences by adding either "other" or "were."

We _____ skipping in the park.

 Jim has lost the _____ sock.

Listen and write.

_____

_____

Read the tricky words and color the flowers using a green pen or pencil.

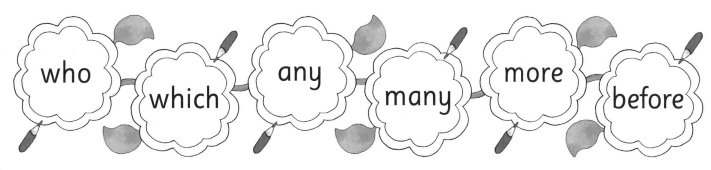

who   which   any   many   more   before

Words and Sentences

What is happening at the park? Choose the right word to complete each of the sentences.

1. The dog is carrying a _____.   stone   stick

2. There is a cat in the _____.   tree   boat

3. The fox is looking at the _____.   cat   rabbit

4. The ducks _____ on the pond.   quack   quit

5. The boys have a bat and _____.   ball   wall

6. The bird in the tree is _____.   singing   swinging

Unit 4

ai, a_e, ay

There are three main ways to write the /ai/ sound. Read the words and then write them in the correct /ai/ spelling.

whale

whale

paint

play

snake

train

tray

name

may   cake

tail

snail   hay

11

because

Tricky Words

want

Write over the dotted letters and add the missing letters.

because b_c___s_ _e___u_e

want   w_nt   _a_t   w_n_

Finish these sentences by adding either "because" or "want."

Do you _____ to help?

He went home _____ he felt sick.

Listen and write.

_____

_____

Write inside the outline letters.

big elephants Catch Ants Under Small elephants.

Words and Sentences

Read each sentence and find the matching picture.

  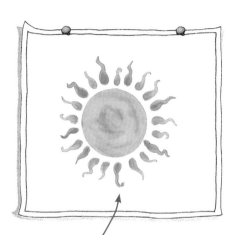

The sun is hot.

I sleep in a bed.

The boat is sailing.

The soap is on the dish.

This sock is long.

He is running.

There are three main ways to write the /ee/ sound.

speed   sneeze   toffee   three

evening   complete   extreme   trapeze

teacher   peanut   peach   teapot

Read the words below and write them in the correct /ee/ spelling.

tea
bee
these
athlete

bee
_____
_____
_____

eve
seal
read
teeth

_____
_____
_____
_____

feet
beak
sleep
theme

_____
_____
_____
_____

saw

Tricky Words

put

Write over the dotted letters and add the missing letters.

saw   s___   _a_   __w

put   p_t   _u_   p__

Finish these sentences by adding either "saw" or "put."

I ____ my drum back in the toy box.

Yesterday, we ____ Dad do a handstand.

Listen and write.

_____

_____

Read the tricky words and color the flowers using a green pen or pencil.

more   before   other   were   because   want

Words and Sentences

Read the phrases and draw a picture for each one.

a rabbit in a hutch

a bat in a tree

a black cat in red boots

three snails in the rain

the moon and some stars

a big rainbow in the sky

Unit 6

There are four main ways to write the /ie/ sound. Read the words and then write them in the correct /ie/ spelling.

light
fly
like
pie
night
prize

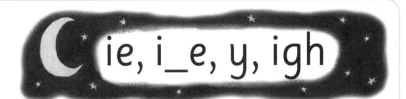

igh

light
_____
_____
_____

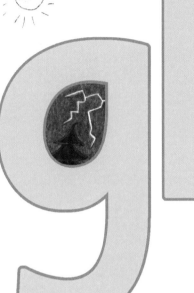

y

_____
_____
_____
_____

lie
time
right
high
reply

ie

_____
_____
_____
_____

_____
_____
_____

i_e

my   die
   kite
sky   tie

17

could

Tricky Words

should

would

Write over the dotted letters and add the missing letters.

could   should   would

c _ _ l d   sho _ _ d   wo _ l _

c _ u _ d   sh _ _ _ d   w _ u _ d

Finish these sentences by adding "could," "should," or "would."

_____ you like some more tea?

I _____ put the tent up now, if you like.

We _____ clean out the hamster's cage.

Listen and write.

_____

_____

_____

Read the tricky words and color the flowers using either green or pink.

other   were   because   want   saw   put

Words and Sentences

Match the two sentences that describe each picture.

I can see a hen. ● ○ He likes to hop.

The oak tree is tall. ○ ○ He has big horns.

The goat is running. ○ ○ It has a brown shell.

A frog is in the pond. ○ ○ They have a bucket.

A snail sits in the rain. ○ ○ Its leaves are green.

The boys play in the sea. ○ ● Her beak is yellow.

Unit 7

There are three main ways to write the /oa/ sound.

coach   float   coast   raincoat

tadpole   home   stone   joke

rainbow   elbow   shadow   window

Read the words below and write them in the correct /oa/ spelling.

those

toast

throw

goat

slow

bone

blow

rose

oak

snow

nose

loaf

20

right   Tricky Words   two   four

Write over the dotted letters and add the missing letters.

right   two   four

r _ _ _ t   t _ _ _   f _ _ _ _

_ _ _ h t   _ _ _ o   _ _ _ _ r

Finish these sentences by adding "right," "two," or "four."

He got all his sums _____.

Two plus two is _____.

The _____ boys are twins.

Listen and write.

_____

_____

_____

Read the tricky words and color the flowers using either green or pink.

want   saw   put   could   should   would

Words and Sentences

Read the sentences and fill in the gaps. Color the pictures to match.

The tall oak _____ is green.

My _____ is long. It has red and black stripes.

My brown _____ has a big collar.

The little green _____ jumped into the pond.

The _____ shines in the night.

I found a _____ in the garden.
It had a yellow shell on its back.

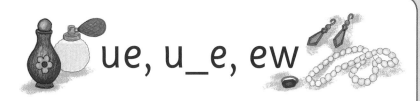

ue, u_e, ew

Read these words. If the /ue/ sound does not work, try the /oo/ sound.

bluebell   argue   untrue   barbecue

ruler   use   excuse   rude

fewer   unscrew   threw   nephew

Read the words below and write them in the correct /ue/ or /oo/ spelling.

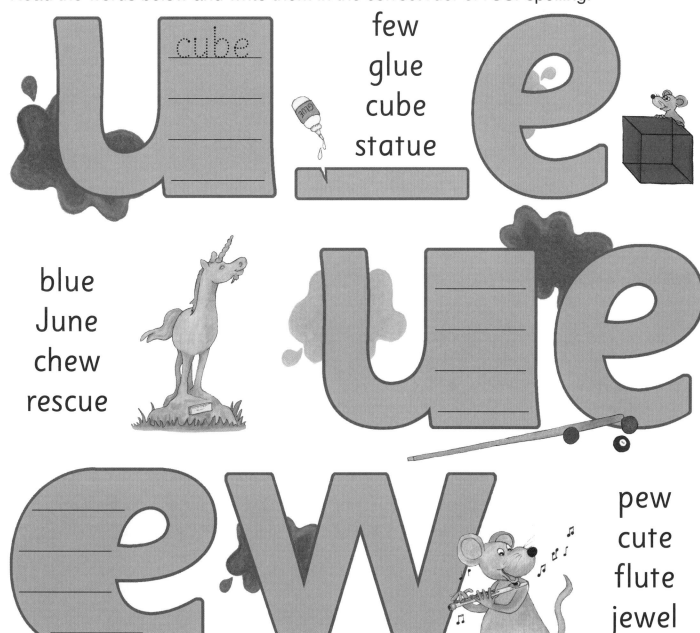

cube

few
glue
cube
statue

blue
June
chew
rescue

pew
cute
flute
jewel

23

 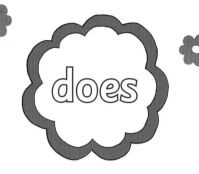 

Tricky Words

Write over the dotted letters and add the missing letters.

goes   g___s   _oe_   g____
does   d___s   _oe_   d____

Finish these sentences by adding "goes" or "does."

He _____ to the park with his sister.

When _____ the match start?

Listen and write.

_____

_____

Read the tricky words and color the flowers using a pink pen or pencil.

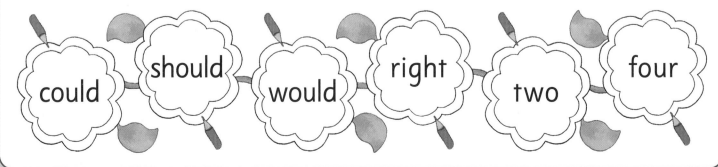

could   should   would   right   two   four

Look at the animals in the zoo and then answer these questions.

1. How many monkeys are in the tree? _____

2. Which animal has a trunk? _____

3. What is the tall bird called? _____

4. Where is the crocodile swimming? _____

5. Who has black and white stripes? _____

6. How many giraffes are there? _____

Make as many words as you can from the letters in the word:

elephants

sleep

_____

_____

_____

_____

_____

_____

Unit 9

ou, ow

There are two main ways to write the /ou/ sound.

loud	about
count	ground
sound	flour

flower	crowd
downhill	growl
shower	vowel

Read the words below and write them in the correct /ou/ spelling.

owl

mouse

brown

mouth

cow

found

cloud

clown

ou

mouse

_____

_____

_____

ow

_____

_____

_____

_____

Tricky Words

made

their

Write over the dotted letters and add the missing letters.

made   m__d_   __a__e   m_____

their   th___r   __ei_   th_____

Finish these sentences by adding "made" or "their."

We _____ some cakes yesterday.

They played with _____ dog.

Listen and write.

_____

_____

Read the tricky words and color the flowers using a pink pen or pencil.

would   right   two   four   goes   does

Words and Sentences

Write a story about a party and draw a picture for each part. Begin by completing the sentences below and then add your own ideas.

We had a party for _____

_____

_____

We ate some _____

_____

_____

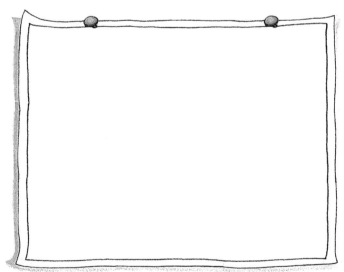

_____

_____

_____

_____

_____

_____

Unit 10

 oi, oy

There are two main ways to write the /oi/ sound.

boil   join
tinfoil   oilcan
ointment   coil

royal   oyster
destroy   employ
annoy   loyal

Read the words below and write them in the correct /oi/ spelling.

coin
____
____
____

joy
coin
boy
spoil

coil
toy
point
enjoy

____
____
____

Tricky Words

Write over the dotted letters and add the missing letters.

once   upon   always

_ n _ _ _   _ _ on   _ _ _ way _ _

_ _ _ _ e   _ p _ _   _ _ l _ _ _ s

Fill in the gaps by adding "once," "upon," or "always," and then finish the story.

_____ _____ a time, there was a

little house in a big wood. The wood was

_____ dark... _____

_____

_____

_____

Read the tricky words and color the flowers using a pink pen or pencil.

two   four   goes   does   made   their

Words and Sentences

Complete the story of Moat Farm, using the words below.

lives　　Neb　Ben　　Farm　　sheep

Green　　sheepdogs　　hill　　truck

1

This is Moat _____ .

2

Farmer Green _____ on Moat Farm.

3

Ben and Neb are _____ .

4

_____ and _____ help on the farm.

5

This morning, Ben and Neb run up the _____ ...

6

...and help round up the _____ .

7

Farmer _____ checks that the sheep are well.

8

Neb and Ben rest in the back of the _____ .

Unit 11

 er, ir, ur

There are three main ways to write the /er/ sound.

butter	helicopter	river	number
third	birthday	twirl	thirsty
purple	Thursday	curl	Saturday

Read the words below and write them in the correct /er/ spelling.

dinner
shirt
purse
letter

er

dinner
_____
_____
_____

bird
fur
sister
girl

hurt
diver
first
turn

32

Write over the dotted letters and add the missing letters.

Finish these sentences by adding "also," "of," or "eight."

There are lots _____ sheep on the farm.

I _____ saw some cows in the barn.

I counted _____ chickens in the yard, too.

Listen and write.

_____

_____

_____

Read the tricky words and color the flowers using either pink or brown.

does   made   their   once   upon   always

Words and Sentences

Read the clues and write the answers in the crossword grid.

ant
hand   tent
doctor egg
soap

map
winter
green
snake
rock
dark

1. This will help you to find your way.
2. If you are sick, you go to see the _____.
3. This small insect lives in a nest underground.
4. If you go camping, you may sleep in this.
5. You wash with _____ and water.
6. This animal hisses.
7. The time of year when it is cold.
8. A chick hatches from this.
9. This is on the end of your arm.
10. A sort of stone.
11. The sky is blue and the trees are _____.
12. At night it is _____.

Unit 12

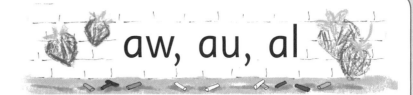

There are three main alternative spellings for the /o/ sound.

yawn   strawberry   shawl   drawing

laundry   August   astronaut   autumn

snowball   chalk   beanstalk   taller

Read the words below and write them in the correct /o/ spelling.

saw
haunt
ball
pause

saw

walk
small
hawk
launch

wall
cause
draw
crawl

35

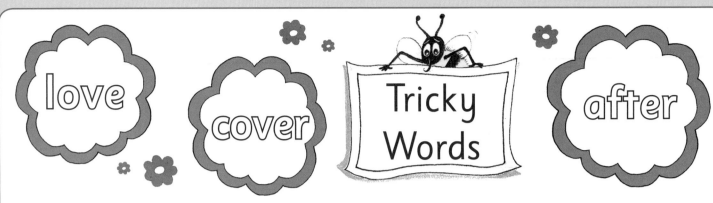

Tricky Words

love cover after

Write over the dotted letters and add the missing letters.

love   cover   after

l __ v __   c __ v __ __   __ f __ e r
l __ __ __   __ __ v __ r   a __ __ e __

Finish these sentences by adding "love," "cover," or "after."

I _____ to go swimming.

_____ lunch, we can play some games.

The _____ of the book was torn.

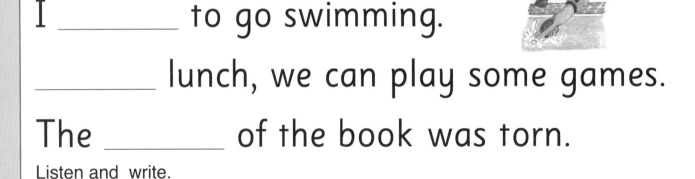

Listen and write.

_____

_____

_____

Read the tricky words and color the flowers using a brown pen or pencil.

once   upon   always   also   of   eight

Words and Sentences

What is happening on the beach? Look carefully and answer the questions below.

1. What are the children doing on the rocks?

_____

2. What can you see in the tide pool?

_____

3. What is on the top of the sandcastle?

_____

4. How many legs does an octopus have?

_____

5. How many beach umbrellas are there?

_____

6. What sort of animal is a seagull?

_____

Unit 13

air, ear, are

The /air/ sound can be written ‹air›, ‹ear›, or ‹are›.

air — air hair chair pair

ear — bear wear tear pear

are — stare rare square dare

Read the words inside the salmon and join them to the right bear. Color the pictures.

Write over the dotted letters and add the missing letters.

every   mother   father

__ v __ __ y   m __ t h __ __   f __ t h __ __

e v __ __ __ __ __   m __ __ __ __ __ __   f __ __ __ __ __

Finish these sentences by adding "every," "mother," or "father."

My _____ and _____ are my parents.

I go dancing _____ week.

Listen and write.

_____

_____

_____

Read the tricky words and color the flowers using a brown pen or pencil.

also   of   eight   love   cover   after

Words and Sentences

Read the story of the midnight feast and answer the questions below.

Once upon a time, there was a king called Alfred. His wife was Queen Matilda. They lived in a castle with a cat called Fluffy.

One night, King Alfred was hungry. So he got up and made himself some cheese sandwiches to eat. Some crumbs from the sandwich fell onto the floor.

A mouse saw the crumbs from her mouse hole in the corner of the room. She could have a midnight feast if she was quick and quiet. She crept out and had just reached the crumbs when Fluffy looked into the room. The mouse ran for her hole as quickly as she could. Fluffy ran for the mouse as quickly as he could.

The mouse reached her hole. She was hungry, but safe!

1. What is the king's name?_____
2. What is the queen's name? _____
3. What sort of animal is Fluffy? _____
4. What did King Alfred make to eat? _____
5. Who saw the crumbs on the floor? _____
6. Who saw the mouse?_____
7. Did the cat catch the mouse? _____

Alternatives

Units 1 to 13 Practice saying the short and long vowel sounds.

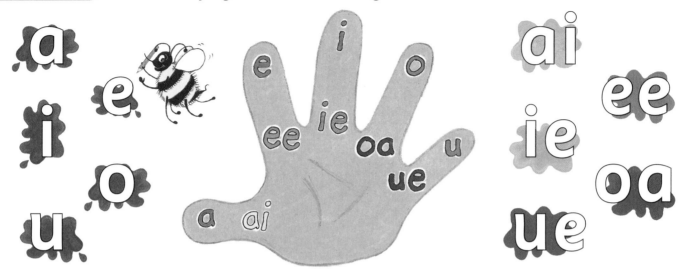

Read each pair of words. Decide which word matches the picture and write it underneath.

ran rain	cot coat	bat bait
	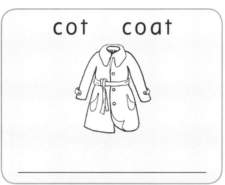	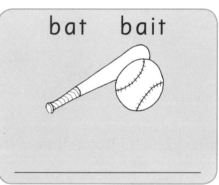
__rain__	_____	_____

rid ride	hug huge	rod road
		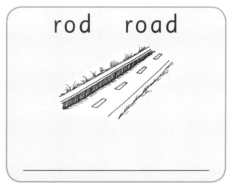
_____	_____	_____

net neat	kit kite	bed bead

_____	_____	_____

Read, Write, and Review

Write inside each lower-case letter and write the capital letter next to it.

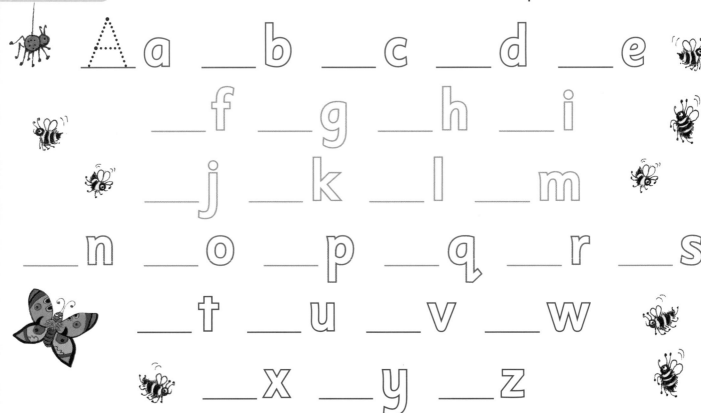

A a __ b __ c __ d __ e

__ f __ g __ h __ i

__ j __ k __ l __ m

__ n __ o __ p __ q __ r __ s

__ t __ u __ v __ w

__ x __ y __ z

Unit 13 Put these letters into alphabetical order.

R j E o

__ __ __ __

N z i U

__ __ __ __

t L a D

__ __ __ __

Read, Write, and Review

Unit 7 Practice writing these digraphs.

oa ·

ng ·

boat   soap   song   ring

Listen and write.

_____

_____

_____

Unit 8 Practice writing these digraphs.

oo ·

or ·

moon   wood   fork   cork

Listen and write.

_____

_____

_____

Read, Write, and Review

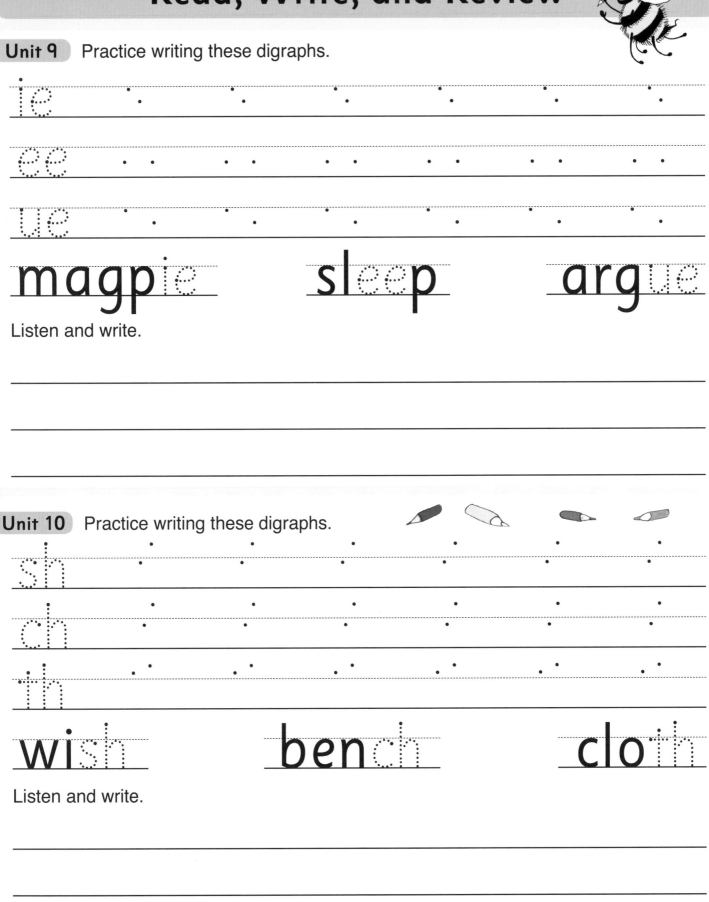

Unit 9 Practice writing these digraphs.

ie

ee

ue

magpie   sleep   argue

Listen and write.

_____

_____

_____

Unit 10 Practice writing these digraphs.

sh

ch

th

wish   bench   cloth

Listen and write.

_____

_____

_____

Read, Write, and Review

Unit 11   Practice writing these digraphs.

er

ar

ai

herd   park   train

Listen and write.

_____

_____

_____

Unit 12   Practice writing these digraphs.

oi

ou

join   spoil   mouth   round

Listen and write.

_____

_____

_____

Tricky Words

Unit 5 Write over the dotted words in the tricky word flowers.
Then find them in the wordsearch.

i	h	m	g	b	e	f	o	r	e
g	l	k	z	e	w	a	n	t	f
b	a	n	y	o	r	s	a	w	k
x	j	d	o	r	e	n	y	b	i
k	i	b	e	c	a	u	s	e	h
v	o	f	x	h	s	w	e	r	e
q	s	m	a	n	y	c	p	u	t
l	e	q	u	d	i	r	m	z	y
j	u	s	m	o	r	e	l	t	a
o	t	h	e	r	k	u	j	i	x

Tricky Words

Unit 9   Write over the dotted words in the tricky word flowers.
Then find them in the wordsearch.

Tricky Words

Unit 13   Write over the dotted words in the tricky word flowers.
Then find them in the wordsearch.

every   once   also   cover

eight   upon   mother   after

of   father   love   always

e	q	u	p	l	o	v	e	s	k
d	c	o	m	f	a	t	h	e	r
o	k	r	e	v	e	r	y	i	g
j	o	f	b	e	i	g	h	t	l
q	u	a	l	w	a	y	s	k	o
s	c	o	v	e	r	l	y	a	b
d	z	a	m	o	t	h	e	r	y
a	f	t	e	r	g	u	p	o	n
z	i	c	h	a	l	s	o	x	e
i	b	r	o	n	c	e	r	y	m